Cookies for Christmas

Publications International, Ltd.

Microwave Cooking: Microwave ovens vary in wattage. Use the cooking times as guidelines and check for doneness before adding more time.

Contents

Kringle's Classics

Chocolate Cherry Treats

½ cup (1 stick) butter, softened
¾ cup firmly packed light brown sugar
¼ cup granulated sugar
½ cup sour cream
1 large egg
1 tablespoon maraschino cherry juice
1 teaspoon vanilla extract
2 cups all-purpose flour
½ teaspoon baking soda
¼ teaspoon salt
1¼ cups "M&M's"® Milk Chocolate Mini
   Baking Bits
½ cup chopped walnuts
⅓ cup well-drained chopped maraschino
   cherries

Preheat oven to 350°F. In large bowl cream butter and sugars until light and fluffy; beat in sour cream, egg, maraschino cherry juice and vanilla. In medium bowl combine flour, baking soda and salt; add to creamed mixture. Stir in "M&M's"® Milk Chocolate Mini Baking Bits, walnuts and maraschino cherries. Drop by heaping tablespoonfuls about 2 inches apart onto ungreased cookie sheets. Bake about 15 minutes. Cool 1 minute on cookie sheets; cool completely on wire racks. Store in tightly covered container.   *Makes 3 dozen cookies*

Buttery Lemon Bars

CRUST
- 1¼ cups all-purpose flour
- ½ cup butter, softened
- ¼ cup powdered sugar
- ½ teaspoon vanilla

FILLING
- 1 cup granulated sugar
- 2 eggs
- ⅓ cup fresh lemon juice
- 2 tablespoons all-purpose flour
- Grated peel of 1 lemon
- Powdered sugar

1. Preheat oven to 350°F.

2. Combine all crust ingredients in small bowl. Beat 2 to 3 minutes until mixture is crumbly. Press onto bottom of ungreased 8-inch square baking pan. Bake 15 to 20 minutes or until edges are lightly browned.

3. Combine all filling ingredients except powdered sugar in small bowl. Beat until well mixed.

4. Pour filling over hot crust. Continue baking 15 to 18 minutes or until filling is set. Sprinkle with powdered sugar; cool completely. Cut into bars; sprinkle again with powdered sugar.

Makes about 16 bars

Fudgy Raisin Pixies

- ½ cup butter, softened
- 2 cups granulated sugar
- 4 eggs
- 2 cups all-purpose flour, divided
- ¾ cup unsweetened cocoa powder
- 2 teaspoons baking powder
- ½ teaspoon salt
- ½ cup chocolate-covered raisins
- Powdered sugar

Beat butter and granulated sugar in large bowl until light and fluffy. Add eggs; mix until well blended. Combine 1 cup flour, cocoa, baking powder and salt in small bowl; add to butter mixture. Mix until well blended. Stir in remaining 1 cup flour and chocolate-covered raisins. Cover; refrigerate until firm, 2 hours or overnight.

Preheat oven to 350°F. Grease cookie sheets. Coat hands with powdered sugar. Shape rounded teaspoonfuls of dough into 1-inch balls; roll in powdered sugar. Place 2 inches apart on prepared cookie sheets. Bake 14 to 17 minutes or until firm to the touch. Remove immediately from cookie sheets; cool completely on wire racks.

Makes about 4 dozen cookies

Alternating from top: Fudgy Raisin Pixies and Buttery Lemon Bars

Santa's Reindeer

½ **cup (1 stick) butter, softened**
⅔ **cup powdered sugar**
¾ **teaspoon vanilla extract**
¾ **cup all-purpose flour**
¼ **cup unsweetened cocoa powder**
1¼ **cups "M&M's"® Milk Chocolate Mini**
    Baking Bits, divided
8 **small pretzel twists, broken in half**
2 **squares (1 ounce) milk chocolate**

Cream butter and sugar until light and fluffy;
beat in vanilla. Combine flour and cocoa
powder; add to creamed mixture. Stir in 1 cup
"M&M's"® Milk Chocolate Mini Baking Bits.
Wrap and chill dough 1 hour. Preheat oven to
300°F. Divide dough into 8 sections. Shape each
section into 4 balls: 1 large, 1 small and 2 very
small for each reindeer. Place large ball on
ungreased cookie sheet; flatten. Place small ball
at bottom of large ball for reindeer snout; flatten.
Place 2 very small balls at top of large ball,
shaping for ears. Press 2 pretzel halves in between
ears for antlers. Bake 18 to 20 minutes. Remove
from oven. Cool on cookie sheets 1 minute; cool
completely on wire racks. Place chocolate in
small microwave-safe bowl. Microwave at HIGH
1 minute; stir. Spread chocolate over cookies.
Decorate with remaining ¼ cup "M&M's"® Milk
Chocolate Mini Baking Bits to make reindeer
faces.   *Makes 8 cookies*

Snowmen

1 **package (20 ounces) refrigerated**
    chocolate chip cookie dough
1½ **cups sifted powdered sugar**
2 **tablespoons milk**
    Candy corn, gum drops, chocolate chips,
    licorice and other assorted small
    candies

1. Preheat oven to 375°F.

2. Cut dough into 12 equal sections. Divide each
section into 3 balls: large, medium and small for
each snowman.

3. For each snowman, place 3 balls in row,
¼ inch apart, on ungreased cookie sheet.

4. Bake 10 to 12 minutes or until edges are very
lightly browned. Cool 4 minutes on cookie
sheets. Remove to wire racks; cool completely.

5. Mix powdered sugar and milk in medium
bowl until smooth. Pour over cookies. Let
cookies stand 20 minutes or until set.

6. Decorate to create faces, hats and arms with
assorted candies.   *Makes 1 dozen cookies*

Elephant Ears

1 package (17¼ ounces) frozen puff pastry, thawed according to package directions
1 egg, beaten
¼ cup sugar, divided
2 squares (1 ounce each) semisweet chocolate

Preheat oven to 375°F. Grease cookie sheets; sprinkle lightly with water. Roll one sheet of pastry to 12×10-inch rectangle. Brush with egg; sprinkle with 1 tablespoon sugar. Tightly roll up 10-inch sides, meeting in center. Brush center with egg and seal rolls tightly together; turn over. Cut into ⅜-inch-thick slices. Place slices on prepared cookie sheets. Sprinkle with 1 tablespoon sugar. Repeat with remaining pastry, egg and sugar. Bake 16 to 18 minutes until golden brown. Remove to wire racks; cool completely.

Melt chocolate in small saucepan over low heat, stirring constantly. Remove from heat. Spread bottoms of cookies with chocolate. Place on wire rack, chocolate side up. Let stand until chocolate is set. Store between layers of waxed paper in airtight containers.

Makes about 4 dozen cookies

Peanut Butter Chocolate Chip Cookies

¼ cup butter or margarine, softened
¼ cup shortening
½ cup REESE'S® Creamy Peanut Butter
½ cup packed light brown sugar
½ cup granulated sugar
1 egg
1¼ cups all-purpose flour
¾ teaspoon baking soda
½ teaspoon baking powder
2 cups (12-ounce package) HERSHEY'S® Semi-Sweet Chocolate Chips
Granulated sugar

1. Heat oven to 375°F.

2. Beat butter, shortening, peanut butter, brown sugar, ½ cup granulated sugar and egg in large bowl until fluffy. Stir together flour, baking soda and baking powder; stir into butter mixture. Stir in chocolate chips (if necessary, work chocolate chips into batter with hands).

3. Shape into 1-inch balls; place on ungreased cookie sheet. With fork dipped in granulated sugar flatten slightly in criss-cross pattern.

4. Bake 9 to 11 minutes or just until set. Cool slightly; remove from cookie sheet to wire rack. Cool completely.

Makes about 3 dozen cookies

Candy Cane Cookies

- 1¼ **cups granulated sugar**
- 1 **Butter Flavor* CRISCO® Stick or 1 cup Butter Flavor CRISCO® all-vegetable shortening**
- 2 **eggs**
- ¼ **cup light corn syrup or regular pancake syrup**
- 1 **tablespoon vanilla**
- 3 **cups plus 4 tablespoons all-purpose flour, divided**
- ¾ **teaspoon baking powder**
- ½ **teaspoon baking soda**
- ½ **teaspoon salt**
- ½ **teaspoon red food color**
- ¼ **teaspoon peppermint extract**

*Butter Flavor Crisco is artificially flavored.

1. Combine sugar and 1 cup shortening in large bowl. Beat at medium speed of electric mixer until well blended. Add eggs, syrup and vanilla. Beat until well blended and fluffy.

2. Combine 3 cups flour, baking powder, baking soda and salt. Add gradually to creamed mixture at low speed. Mix until well blended.

3. Divide dough in half. Add red food color and peppermint extract to one half. Wrap each half in plastic wrap. Refrigerate several hours or overnight.

4. Heat oven to 375°F. Place sheets of foil on countertop for cooling cookies.

5. Roll 1 rounded teaspoonful plain dough with hands into a 6-inch rope on lightly floured surface. Repeat, using 1 teaspoonful red dough. Place ropes side by side. Twist together gently. Pinch ends to seal. Curve one end into the "hook" of a candy cane. Transfer to ungreased baking sheet with large pancake turner. Repeat with remaining dough. Place cookies 2 inches apart.

6. Bake one baking sheet at a time at 375°F for 7 to 9 minutes, or until just lightly browned. *Do not overbake.* Cool 2 minutes on baking sheet. Remove cookies to foil to cool completely.
Makes about 4½ dozen cookies

Helpful Hint

Store soft and crisp cookies separately at room temperature to prevent changes in texture and flavor. Keep soft cookies in airtight containers and store crisp cookies in containers with loose fitting lids.

Hanukkah Coin Cookies

**1 cup (2 sticks) butter or margarine,
    softened**
1 cup sugar
1 egg
1 teaspoon vanilla extract
1¾ cups all-purpose flour
½ cup HERSHEY'S Cocoa
1½ teaspoons baking powder
½ teaspoon salt
Buttercream Frosting (recipe follows)

1. Beat butter, sugar, egg and vanilla in large bowl until well blended. Stir together flour, cocoa, baking powder and salt; gradually add to butter mixture, beating until well blended. Divide dough in half; place each half on separate sheet of wax paper.

2. Shape each portion into log, about 7 inches long. Wrap each log in wax paper or plastic wrap. Refrigerate until firm, at least 8 hours.

3. Heat oven to 325°F. Cut logs into ¼-inch-thick slices. Place on ungreased cookie sheet.

4. Bake 8 to 10 minutes or until set. Cool slightly; remove from cookie sheet to wire rack. Cool completely. Prepare Buttercream Frosting; spread over tops of cookies.
Makes about 4½ dozen cookies

Buttercream Frosting

¼ cup (½ stick) butter, softened
1½ cups powdered sugar
1 to 2 tablespoons milk
½ teaspoon vanilla extract
Yellow food color

1. Beat butter until creamy. Gradually add powdered sugar and milk to butter, beating to desired consistency. Stir in vanilla and food color.
Makes about 1 cup frosting

Helpful Hint

Refrigerator doughs, like this one, are perfect for preparing ahead of time. Tightly wrapped rolls of dough can be stored in the refrigerator for up to one week, or frozen for up to six weeks. Then the dough is ready to be sliced and baked at a moment's notice.

14

Homemade Coconut Macaroons

3 egg whites
¼ teaspoon cream of tartar
⅛ teaspoon salt
¾ cup sugar
2¼ cups shredded coconut, toasted*
1 teaspoon vanilla extract

To toast coconut, spread evenly on cookie sheet. Toast in preheated 350°F oven 7 minutes. Stir and toast 1 to 2 minutes more or until light golden brown.

Preheat oven to 325°F. Line cookie sheets with parchment paper or foil. Beat egg whites, cream of tartar and salt in large bowl with electric mixer until soft peaks form. Beat in sugar, 1 tablespoon at a time, until egg whites are stiff and shiny. Fold in coconut and vanilla. Drop tablespoonfuls of dough 4 inches apart onto prepared cookie sheets; spread each into 3-inch circles with back of spoon.

Bake 18 to 22 minutes until light brown. Cool 1 minute on cookie sheets. Remove to wire racks; cool completely. Store in airtight container.   *Makes about 2 dozen cookies*

Honey Spice Balls

½ cup butter, softened
½ cup packed brown sugar
1 egg
1 tablespoon honey
1 teaspoon vanilla extract
2 cups all-purpose flour
½ teaspoon baking powder
½ teaspoon ground cinnamon
¼ teaspoon ground nutmeg
Uncooked quick oats

Preheat oven to 350°F. Grease cookie sheets. Beat butter and brown sugar in large bowl with electric mixer until creamy. Add egg, honey and vanilla; beat until light and fluffy. Stir in flour, baking powder, cinnamon and nutmeg until well blended. Shape tablespoonfuls of dough into balls; roll in oats. Place 2 inches apart on prepared cookie sheets.

Bake 15 to 18 minutes until cookie tops crack slightly. Cool 1 minute on cookie sheets. Remove to wire racks; cool completely. Store in airtight container.

Makes about 2½ dozen cookies

Top left to bottom right: Homemade Coconut Macaroons and Honey Spice Balls

Mexican Wedding Cookies

1 cup pecan pieces or halves
1 cup butter, softened
2 cups powdered sugar, divided
2 cups all-purpose flour, divided
2 teaspoons vanilla
⅛ teaspoon salt

1. Place pecans in food processor. Process using on/off pulsing action until pecans are ground, but not pasty.

2. Beat butter and ½ cup powdered sugar in large bowl until light and fluffy. Gradually add 1 cup flour, vanilla and salt. Beat until well blended. Stir in remaining 1 cup flour and ground nuts. Shape dough into ball; wrap in plastic wrap and refrigerate 1 hour or until firm.

3. Preheat oven to 350°F. Shape tablespoonfuls of dough into 1-inch balls. Place 1 inch apart on ungreased cookie sheets. Bake 12 to 15 minutes or until pale golden brown. Let cookies stand on cookie sheets 2 minutes.

4. Place 1 cup powdered sugar in 13×9-inch glass dish. Roll hot cookies in powdered sugar, coating well. Let cookies cool in sugar.

5. Sift remaining ½ cup powdered sugar over sugar-coated cookies before serving. Store tightly covered at room temperature.

Makes about 4 dozen cookies

Chocolate Spritz Cookies

1 package DUNCAN HINES® Golden Sugar Cookie Mix
⅓ cup unsweetened cocoa powder
1 egg
⅓ cup vegetable oil
2 tablespoons water

1. Preheat oven to 375°F.

2. Combine cookie mix and cocoa in large mixing bowl. Stir until blended. Add egg, oil and water. Stir until thoroughly blended.

3. Fill cookie press with dough. Press desired shapes 2 inches apart onto ungreased cookie sheets. Bake at 375°F for 6 to 8 minutes or until set. Cool 1 minute on baking sheets. Remove to cooling racks. Cool completely.

Makes 5 to 6 dozen cookies

Note: For a delicious no-cholesterol variation, substitute 2 egg whites for whole egg.

Helpful Hint

For festive cookies, decorate before baking with assorted decors, or after baking with melted milk chocolate or semi-sweet chocolate, or white chocolate and chopped nuts.

Oatmeal Raisin Cookies

¾ **cup all-purpose flour**
¾ **teaspoon salt**
½ **teaspoon baking soda**
½ **teaspoon ground cinnamon**
¾ **cup butter, softened**
¾ **cup granulated sugar**
¾ **cup packed light brown sugar**
1 **egg**
1 **tablespoon water**
3 **teaspoons vanilla, divided**
3 **cups uncooked old-fashioned or**
    quick-cooking oats
1 **cup raisins**
½ **cup powdered sugar (optional)**
1 **tablespoon milk (optional)**

1. Preheat oven to 375°F. Grease cookie sheets; set aside. Combine flour, salt, baking soda and cinnamon in small bowl.

2. Beat butter, granulated sugar and brown sugar in large bowl until light and fluffy. Add egg, water and 2 teaspoons vanilla; beat well. Add flour mixture; beat just until blended. Stir in oats and raisins.

3. Drop tablespoonfuls of dough 2 inches apart onto prepared cookie sheets.

4. Bake 10 to 11 minutes or until edges are golden brown. Let cookies stand 2 minutes on cookie sheets; transfer to wire racks to cool.

5. For glaze, stir powdered sugar, milk and remaining 1 teaspoon vanilla in small bowl until smooth. Drizzle over cookies with fork or spoon, if desired. Store cookies tightly covered at room temperature or freeze up to 3 months.

Makes about 4 dozen cookies

Helpful Hint

Most cookies bake quickly and should be watched carefully to avoid overbaking. Check them at the minimum baking time, then watch carefully to make sure they don't burn. It is generally better to slightly underbake rather than to overbake cookies.

Peanut Butter Crackles

- 1½ cups all-purpose flour
- 1 teaspoon baking soda
- ⅛ teaspoon salt
- ½ cup (1 stick) margarine or butter, softened
- ½ cup SKIPPY® Creamy or SUPER CHUNK® Peanut Butter
- ½ cup granulated sugar
- ½ cup packed brown sugar
- 1 egg
- 1 teaspoon vanilla
  Granulated sugar
  Chocolate candy kisses

1. Preheat oven to 375°F. In small bowl, combine flour, baking soda and salt; set aside.

2. In large bowl, beat margarine and peanut butter until smooth. Beat in sugars until blended. Beat in egg and vanilla. Gradually beat in flour mixture until well mixed.

3. Shape dough into 1-inch balls. Roll in granulated sugar. Place 2 inches apart on ungreased cookie sheets.

4. Bake 10 minutes or until lightly browned. Remove from oven and quickly press chocolate candy kiss firmly into top of each cookie (cookie will crack around edges). Remove to wire racks to cool completely.

Makes about 5 dozen cookies

Chocolate Chip Cookies

- 8 tablespoons margarine, softened
- 1½ cups packed light brown sugar
- 2 egg whites
- 1 teaspoon vanilla
- 2½ cups all-purpose flour
- 1½ teaspoons baking soda
- ½ teaspoon salt
- ⅓ cup skim milk
- ¾ cup (4 ounces) semisweet chocolate chips
- ½ cup chopped pecans or walnuts (optional)

1. Preheat oven to 350°F. Spray cookie sheets with nonstick cooking spray.

2. Beat margarine and brown sugar in large bowl until fluffy. Beat in egg whites and vanilla.

3. Combine flour, baking soda and salt in medium bowl. Add flour mixture to margarine mixture alternately with milk, ending with flour mixture. Stir in chocolate chips and pecans, if desired.

4. Drop dough by slightly rounded tablespoonfuls onto prepared cookie sheets. Bake about 10 minutes or until lightly browned. Cool on wire racks. *Makes about 6 dozen cookies*

Almond-Orange Shortbread

1 cup (4 ounces) sliced almonds, divided
2 cups all-purpose flour
1 cup cold butter, cut into pieces
½ cup sugar
½ cup cornstarch
2 tablespoons grated orange peel
1 teaspoon almond extract

1. Preheat oven to 350°F. To toast almonds, spread ¾ cup almonds in single layer in large baking pan. Bake 6 minutes or until golden brown, stirring frequently. Remove almonds from oven. Cool completely in pan. *Reduce oven temperature to 325°F.*

2. Place toasted almonds in food processor. Process using on/off pulsing action until coarsely chopped.

3. Add flour, butter, sugar, cornstarch, orange peel and almond extract to food processor. Process using on/off pulsing action until mixture resembles coarse crumbs.

4. Press dough firmly and evenly into 10×8½-inch rectangle on large ungreased cookie sheet. Score dough into 1¼-inch squares with knife. Press one slice of remaining ¼ cup almonds in center of each square.

5. Bake 30 to 40 minutes or until shortbread is firm when pressed and lightly browned.

6. Immediately cut into squares along score lines with sharp knife. Remove cookies with spatula to wire racks; cool completely.

7. Store loosely covered at room temperature up to 1 week. *Makes about 5 dozen cookies*

Helpful Hint

Try cutting bar cookies into triangles or diamonds for a festive new shape. To make serving easy, remove a corner piece first; then remove the rest.

Cookie Cutter Favorites

Gingerbread Cookies

- ¾ **cup light or dark molasses**
- ¾ **cup margarine or butter**
- ¾ **cup packed light brown sugar**
- 4½ **cups all-purpose flour**
- 1 **tablespoon ground ginger**
- 2 **teaspoons ground cinnamon**
- 1 **teaspoon DAVIS® Baking Powder**
- ½ **teaspoon baking soda**
- ½ **teaspoon ground nutmeg**
- ¼ **cup egg substitute**
  Decorator icing, raisins and assorted candies, optional

1. Heat molasses, margarine or butter and brown sugar in saucepan over medium heat to a boil, stirring occasionally. Remove from heat; cool.

2. Mix flour, ginger, cinnamon, baking powder, baking soda and nutmeg in large bowl. Blend egg substitute into molasses mixture. Stir molasses mixture into flour mixture until smooth. Wrap dough; refrigerate 1 hour.

3. Divide dough in half. Roll dough to ¼-inch thickness on floured surface. Cut with floured 5×3-inch gingerbread people cutters. Place on lightly greased baking sheets.

4. Bake in preheated 350°F oven for 10 to 12 minutes or until lightly browned. Remove from sheets; cool on wire racks. Decorate as desired. *Makes 2 dozen cookies*

24

Christmas Ornament Cookies

- 2¼ **cups all-purpose flour**
- ¼ **teaspoon salt**
- 1 **cup sugar**
- ¾ **cup butter, softened**
- 1 **large egg**
- 1 **teaspoon vanilla**
- 1 **teaspoon almond extract**
  Icing (recipe follows)
  Assorted candies or decors

Place flour and salt in medium bowl; stir to combine. Beat sugar and butter in large bowl until light and fluffy. Beat in egg, vanilla and almond extract. Gradually add flour mixture. Beat until well blended. Divide dough in half; cover and refrigerate 30 minutes or until firm.

Preheat oven to 350°F. Working with 1 portion at a time, roll out dough on lightly floured surface to ¼-inch thickness. Cut dough into desired shapes with assorted floured cookie cutters. Reroll trimmings and cut out more cookies. Place cutouts on ungreased baking sheets. Using drinking straw or tip of sharp knife, cut hole near top of each cookie to allow for piece of ribbon or string to be inserted for hanger. Bake 10 to 12 minutes or until edges are golden brown. Let cookies stand on baking sheets 1 minute. Remove cookies to wire racks; cool completely.

Prepare Icing. Spoon Icing into small resealable plastic food storage bag. Cut off very tiny corner of bag; pipe Icing decoratively on cookies. Decorate with candies as desired. Let stand at room temperature 40 minutes or until set. Thread ribbon through each cookie hole to hang as Christmas tree ornaments.

Makes about 2 dozen cookies

Icing

- 2 **cups powdered sugar**
- 2 **tablespoons milk or lemon juice**
  Food coloring (optional)

Place powdered sugar and milk in small bowl; stir with spoon until smooth. (Icing will be very thick. If it is too thick, stir in 1 teaspoon additional milk.) Divide into small bowls and tint with food coloring, if desired.

Festive Rugelach

- **1½ cups (3 sticks) butter or margarine, softened**
- **12 ounces cream cheese, softened**
- **3½ cups all-purpose flour, divided**
- **½ cup powdered sugar**
- **¾ cup granulated sugar**
- **1½ teaspoons ground cinnamon**
- **1¾ cups "M&M's"® Chocolate Mini Baking Bits, divided**
- **Powdered sugar**

Preheat oven to 350°F. Lightly grease cookie sheets; set aside. In large bowl cream butter and cream cheese. Slowly work in 3 cups flour. Divide dough into 6 equal pieces and shape into squares. Lightly flour dough, wrap in waxed paper and refrigerate at least 1 hour. Combine remaining ½ cup all-purpose flour and ½ cup powdered sugar. Remove one piece of dough at a time from refrigerator; roll out on surface dusted with flour-sugar mixture to 18×5×⅛-inch-thick strip. Combine granulated sugar and cinnamon. Sprinkle dough strip with about 2 tablespoons cinnamon-sugar mixture. Sprinkle about ¼ cup "M&M's"® Chocolate Mini Baking Bits on wide end of each strip. Roll dough strip starting at wide end to completely enclose baking bits. Slice strip into 1½-inch lengths; place seam-side down about 2 inches apart on prepared cookie sheets. Repeat with remaining ingredients. Bake 16 to 18 minutes or until golden. Cool completely on wire racks. Sprinkle with powdered sugar. Store in tightly covered container. *Makes about 6 dozen cookies*

Variation: For crescent shapes, roll each piece of dough into 12-inch circle. Sprinkle with cinnamon-sugar mixture. Cut into 12 wedges. Place about ½ teaspoon "M&M's"® Chocolate Mini Baking Bits at wide end of each wedge and roll up to enclose baking bits. Place seam-side down on prepared baking sheet and proceed as directed.

Helpful Hint

To easily soften butter in your microwave, place 1 stick of butter on a microwavable plate and heat at LOW (30% power) for about 30 seconds or just until softened.

Chocolate Reindeer

1 cup butter, softened
1 cup granulated sugar
1 egg
1 teaspoon vanilla
2 ounces semisweet chocolate, melted
2¼ cups all-purpose flour
1 teaspoon baking powder
¼ teaspoon salt
Royal Icing (recipe follows)
Assorted small candies

1. Beat butter and sugar in large bowl at high speed of electric mixer until fluffy. Beat in egg and vanilla. Add melted chocolate; mix well. Add flour, baking powder and salt; mix well. Wrap dough in plastic wrap and refrigerate about 2 hours or until firm.

2. Preheat oven to 325°F. Grease 2 cookie sheets; set aside.

3. Divide dough in half. Reserve 1 half; refrigerate remaining half.

4. Roll reserved dough on well-floured surface to ¼-inch thickness. Cut with reindeer cookie cutter. Place 2 inches apart on prepared cookie sheets. Chill 10 minutes.

5. Bake 13 to 15 minutes or until set. Cool completely on cookie sheets. Repeat steps with remaining dough.

6. Prepare Royal Icing.

7. To decorate, pipe assorted colored icing on reindeer and add small candies. For best results, let cookies dry overnight uncovered before storing in airtight container at room temperature. *Makes 16 (4-inch) cookies*

Royal Icing

2 to 3 large egg whites*
2 to 4 cups powdered sugar
1 tablespoon lemon juice
Assorted food colors

Use only grade A clean, uncracked eggs.

Beat 2 egg whites in medium bowl with electric mixer until peaks just begin to hold their shape. Add 2 cups powdered sugar and lemon juice; beat for 1 minute. If consistency is too thin for piping, gradually add more sugar until desired result is achieved; if it is too thick, add another egg white. Divide icing among several small bowls and tint to desired colors. Keep bowls tightly covered until ready to use.

Holiday Sugar Cookies

1 cup butter, softened
¾ cup sugar
1 egg
2 cups all-purpose flour
1 teaspoon baking powder
¼ teaspoon salt
¼ teaspoon ground cinnamon
Colored sprinkles or sugars (optional)

Beat butter and sugar in large bowl with electric mixer until creamy. Add egg; beat until fluffy.

Stir in flour, baking powder, salt and cinnamon until well blended. Form dough into a ball; wrap in plastic wrap and flatten. Refrigerate about 2 hours or until firm.

Preheat oven to 350°F. Roll out dough, small portion at a time, to ¼-inch thickness on lightly floured surface with lightly floured rolling pin. (Keep remaining dough wrapped in refrigerator.)

Cut out cookies with 3-inch cookie cutters. Sprinkle with colored sprinkles or sugars, if desired. Transfer to ungreased cookie sheets.

Bake 7 to 9 minutes until edges are lightly browned. Let cookies stand on cookie sheets 1 minute; transfer to wire racks to cool completely. Store in airtight container.

Makes about 3 dozen cookies

European Kolacky

1 cup butter or margarine, softened
1 package (8 ounces) cream cheese, softened
1 tablespoon milk
1 tablespoon sugar
1 egg yolk
1½ cups all-purpose flour
½ teaspoon baking powder
1 can SOLO® or 1 jar BAKER® Filling (any flavor)
Powdered sugar

Beat butter, cream cheese, milk and sugar in medium bowl with electric mixer until thoroughly blended. Beat in egg yolk. Sift together flour and baking powder; stir into butter mixture to make stiff dough. Cover and refrigerate several hours or overnight.

Preheat oven to 400°F. Roll out dough on lightly floured surface to ¼-inch thickness. Cut dough with floured 2-inch cookie cutter. Place cookies on ungreased cookie sheets about 1 inch apart. Make depression in centers of cookies with thumb or back of spoon. Spoon 1 teaspoon filling into centers of cookies.

Bake 10 to 12 minutes or until lightly browned. Remove from baking sheets and cool completely on wire racks. Sprinkle with powdered sugar just before serving. *Makes about 3 dozen cookies*

Spicy Gingerbread Cookies

COOKIES

- ½ **cup packed brown sugar**
- ¾ **cup (1½ sticks) butter, softened**
- ⅔ **cup light molasses**
- 1 **egg**
- 1½ **teaspoons grated lemon peel**
- 2½ **cups all-purpose flour**
- 1¼ **teaspoons ground cinnamon**
- 1 **teaspoon ground allspice**
- 1 **teaspoon vanilla**
- ½ **teaspoon baking soda**
- ½ **teaspoon salt**
- ½ **teaspoon ground ginger**
- ¼ **teaspoon baking powder**

FROSTING

- 4 **cups powdered sugar**
- ½ **cup (1 stick) butter, softened**
- 4 **tablespoons milk**
- 2 **teaspoons vanilla**
  Food colors (optional)

For cookies, combine brown sugar, butter, molasses, egg and lemon peel in large bowl. Beat at medium speed of electric mixer until smooth and creamy. Add remaining cookie ingredients. Reduce speed to low; beat well. Cover; refrigerate at least 2 hours.

Preheat oven to 350°F. Lightly grease cookie sheets; set aside. Roll out dough, half at a time, on well floured surface to ¼-inch thickness. (Keep remaining dough refrigerated.) Cut with 3- to 4-inch cookie cutters. Place on prepared cookie sheets. Bake 6 to 8 minutes or until no indentation remains when touched. Remove immediately. Cool completely.

For frosting, combine powdered sugar, butter, milk and vanilla in small bowl. Beat at low speed of electric mixer until fluffy. Tint frosting with food colors, if desired. Decorate cookies with frosting. *Makes about 4 dozen cookies*

Helpful Hint

To get bright colors and to keep frosting at the proper consistency, tint frosting with paste food colors. Add a small amount of the paste color with a toothpick, then stir well. Slowly add more color until the frosting is the desired shade. If you use liquid food colors and the frosting becomes too thin, add more powdered sugar, beating until the desired consistency is reached.

Glazed Sugar Cookies

COOKIES

- 1 package DUNCAN HINES® Golden Sugar Cookie Mix
- 1 egg
- ¼ cup vegetable oil
- 1 teaspoon water

GLAZE

- 1½ cups sifted confectioners' sugar
- 2 to 3 tablespoons water or milk
- ¾ teaspoon vanilla extract
  Food coloring (optional)
  Red and green sugar crystals, nonpareils or cinnamon candies

Preheat oven to 375°F.

Combine cookie mix, egg, oil and 1 teaspoon water in large bowl. Stir until thoroughly blended. Roll dough to ¼-inch thickness on lightly floured surface. Cut dough into desired shapes using floured cookie cutters. Place cookies 2 inches apart on *ungreased* cookie sheets. Bake 7 to 8 minutes or until edges are light golden brown. Cool 1 minute on baking sheets. Remove to cooling racks. Cool completely.

Combine sugar, 2 to 3 tablespoons water and vanilla extract in medium bowl. Beat until smooth. Tint glaze with food coloring, if desired. Brush glaze on each cookie with clean pastry brush. Sprinkle cookies with sugar crystals, nonpareils or cinnamon candies before glaze sets. Allow glaze to set before storing between layers of waxed paper in airtight container.

Makes 4 dozen cookies

Helpful Hint

Use DUNCAN HINES® Vanilla Frosting for a quick glaze. Heat frosting in opened container in microwave oven at HIGH for 10 to 15 seconds. Stir well. Spread on cookies and decorate as desired before frosting sets.

Dutch St. Nicolas Cookies

½ **cup whole natural almonds**
¾ **cup butter or margarine, softened**
½ **cup packed brown sugar**
2 **tablespoons milk**
1½ **teaspoons ground cinnamon**
¼ **teaspoon ground nutmeg**
¼ **teaspoon ground ginger**
¼ **teaspoon ground cloves**
2 **cups sifted all-purpose flour**
1½ **teaspoons baking powder**
½ **teaspoon salt**
¼ **cup coarsely chopped citron**

Spread almonds in single layer on baking sheet. Bake at 375°F, 10 to 12 minutes, stirring occasionally, until lightly toasted. Cool. Chop finely. In large bowl, cream butter, sugar, milk and spices. In small bowl, combine flour, baking powder and salt. Add flour mixture to creamed mixture; blend well. Stir in almonds and citron. Knead dough slightly to make ball. Cover; refrigerate until firm. Roll out dough ¼ inch thick on lightly floured surface. Cut out with cookie cutters. Place 2 inches apart on greased cookie sheets. Bake at 375°F, 7 to 10 minutes, until lightly browned. Remove to wire racks to cool. *Makes about 3½ dozen cookies*

Favorite recipe from **Almond Board of California**

Holiday Chocolate Shortbread Cookies

1 **cup (2 sticks) butter, softened**
1¼ **cups powdered sugar**
1 **teaspoon vanilla extract**
½ **cup HERSHEY'S Dutch Processed Cocoa or HERSHEY'S Cocoa**
1¾ **cups all-purpose flour**
1⅔ **cups (10-ounce package) HERSHEY'S Premier White Chips**

1. Heat oven to 300°F. Beat butter, powdered sugar and vanilla in large bowl until creamy. Add cocoa; beat until well blended. Gradually add flour, stirring until smooth.

2. Roll or pat dough to ¼-inch thickness on lightly floured surface or between 2 pieces of wax paper. Cut into holiday shapes using star, tree, wreath or other cookie cutters. Reroll dough scraps, cutting cookies until dough is used. Place on ungreased cookie sheet.

3. Bake 15 to 20 minutes or just until firm. Immediately place white chips, flat side down, in decorative design on warm cookies. Cool slightly; remove from cookie sheet to wire rack. Cool completely. Store in airtight container. *Makes about 4½ dozen cookies*

Note: For more even baking, place similar shapes and sizes of cookies on same cookie sheet.

Orange-Almond Sables

1½ cups powdered sugar
1 cup butter, softened
1 tablespoon finely grated orange peel
1 tablespoon almond-flavored liqueur *or*
1 teaspoon almond extract
¾ cup whole blanched almonds, toasted*
1¾ to 2 cups all-purpose flour
¼ teaspoon salt
1 large egg, beaten

*To toast almonds, spread in single layer on baking sheet. Bake in preheated 350°F oven 8 to 10 minutes or until brown, stirring twice.

Preheat oven to 375°F. Beat powdered sugar and butter in bowl until fluffy. Beat in orange peel and liqueur. Reserve 24 whole almonds. Process remaining cooled almonds in food processor using on/off pulsing action until ground, but not pasty. Mix ground almonds, flour and salt in medium bowl; add to butter mixture. Beat until well blended. Roll out dough on floured surface to ¼-inch thickness. Cut with floured 2½-inch fluted or round cookie cutter. Place 2 inches apart on ungreased cookie sheets. Brush with beaten egg. Press 1 whole reserved almond in each cookie center. Brush almond with beaten egg. Bake cookies 10 to 12 minutes or until golden. Stand 1 minute on cookie sheets. Remove to wire racks; cool completely.

Makes about 2 dozen cookies

Berry Treasures

2½ cups all-purpose flour
½ cup sugar
⅔ cup butter
1 egg
½ teaspoon salt
¼ teaspoon baking soda
2 tablespoons milk
1½ teaspoons vanilla
¾ cup mixed berry preserves
Additional sugar

1. Preheat oven to 350°F. Combine flour, sugar, butter, egg, salt, baking soda, milk and vanilla in large bowl. Beat 3 to 4 minutes, scraping bowl often, until well mixed.

2. Roll out dough, ½ at a time, to ⅛-inch thickness on well-floured surface. Cut out cookies with 2½-inch round cookie cutter. Place ½ of cookies 2 inches apart on ungreased cookie sheets; place level teaspoonful preserves in center of each cookie.

3. Make small "X" or cutout with very small cookie cutter in top of each remaining cookie. Place over preserves; press edges together with fork. Sprinkle with sugar.

4. Bake 11 to 13 minutes or until edges are very lightly browned. Remove cookies immediately to wire racks to cool completely.

Makes about 2 dozen sandwich cookies

3-D Holiday Cookies

- ½ **cup (1 stick) butter, softened**
- ⅓ **cup granulated sugar**
- 2 **tablespoons firmly packed light brown sugar**
- 1 **large egg**
- ½ **teaspoon vanilla extract**
- 1½ **cups all-purpose flour**
- ½ **teaspoon baking powder**
- ⅛ **teaspoon salt**
   Decorating Glaze (recipe follows)
   Assorted food colorings
- ½ **cup "M&M's"® Chocolate Mini Baking Bits**

In large bowl cream butter and sugars until light and fluffy; beat in egg and vanilla. In small bowl combine flour, baking powder and salt; blend into creamed mixture. Wrap and refrigerate dough 2 to 3 hours. Preheat oven to 375°F. Working with half of dough at a time on lightly floured surface, roll to ⅛-inch thickness. Cut into pairs of desired shapes using 3-inch cookie cutters. Reroll trimmings and cut out more pairs. Place cutouts 1 inch apart on ungreased cookie sheets. Bake 5 to 7 minutes. Immediately cut 1 cookie of each pair in half vertically. Cool on cookie sheets 1 minute; cool completely on wire racks. Prepare Decorating Glaze. Tint glaze with food colorings as desired. Spread line of glaze down cut edge of half cookie. Press half cookie

to middle of whole cookie; let set. Repeat with remaining half cookie, attaching half cookie to middle back of whole cookie. Spread glaze over entire 3-D cookies; let set. Using glaze to attach, decorate cookies with "M&M's"® Chocolate Mini Baking Bits. Store in tightly covered container. *Makes 18 (3-D) cookies*

Decorating Glaze: In large bowl combine 4 cups powdered sugar and ¼ cup water until smooth. If necessary, add additional water, 1 teaspoon at a time, to make a medium-thick pourable glaze.

Helpful Hint

For even baking and browning of cookies, bake them in the center of the oven. If the heat distribution in your oven is uneven, turn the cookie sheet halfway through the baking time.

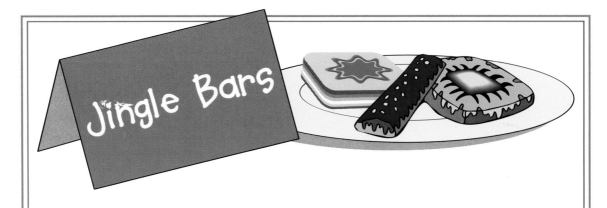

Jingle Bars

Chocolate Chip Walnut Bars

Bar Cookie Crust (page 44)
2 **eggs**
½ **cup KARO® Light or Dark Corn Syrup**
½ **cup sugar**
2 **tablespoons margarine or butter, melted**
1 **cup (6 ounces) semisweet chocolate chips**
¾ **cup chopped walnuts**

1. Preheat oven to 350°F. Prepare Bar Cookie Crust.

2. Meanwhile, in medium bowl beat eggs, corn syrup, sugar and margarine until well blended. Stir in chocolate chips and walnuts. Pour over hot crust; spread evenly.

3. Bake 15 to 18 minutes or until set. Cool completely on wire rack. Cut into 2×1½-inch bars. *Makes about 32 bars*

Helpful Hint

When baking bar cookies, always use the pan size specified in the recipe to make sure that they bake to the proper texture. If using a glass baking dish instead of a metal baking pan, reduce the oven temperature by 25°F.

Top to bottom: Pecan Pie Bars (page 44), Almond Toffee Triangles (page 56) and Chocolate Chip Walnut Bars

Pecan Pie Bars

Bar Cookie Crust (recipe follows)
2 eggs
¾ cup KARO® Light or Dark Corn Syrup
¾ cup sugar
2 tablespoons margarine or butter, melted
1 teaspoon vanilla
1¼ cups coarsely chopped pecans

1. Preheat oven to 350°F. Prepare Bar Cookie Crust.

2. Meanwhile, in large bowl beat eggs, corn syrup, sugar, margarine and vanilla until well blended. Stir in pecans. Pour over hot crust; spread evenly.

3. Bake 20 minutes or until filling is firm around edges and slightly firm in center. Cool completely on wire rack. Cut into 2×1½-inch bars.   *Makes about 32 bars*

Chocolate Pecan Pie Bars: Follow recipe for Pecan Pie Bars. Add ½ cup (3 ounces) semisweet chocolate, melted, to egg mixture. Complete as recipe directs.

Bar Cookie Crust

MAZOLA NO STICK® Cooking Spray
2 cups flour
½ cup (1 stick) cold margarine or butter, cut into pieces
⅓ cup sugar
¼ teaspoon salt

1. Preheat oven to 350°F. Spray 13×9-inch baking pan with cooking spray.

2. In large bowl with mixer at medium speed, beat flour, margarine, sugar and salt until mixture resembles coarse crumbs. Press firmly into bottom and ¼ inch up sides of prepared baking pan.

3. Bake 15 minutes or until golden brown. Top with desired filling. Complete as recipe directs.

Helpful Hint

For easy removal of bar cookies (and no cleanup!), line the baking pan with foil and leave at least 3 inches hanging over on each end. Grease the foil if directed to grease the pan in the recipe. Use the foil to lift out the bars, place them on a cutting board and carefully remove the foil. Then simply cut the treats into pieces.

Carrot & Spice Bars

1 cup low-fat (1%) milk
¼ cup butter, melted
1 cup bran flakes cereal
2 eggs
1 jar (2½ ounces) puréed baby food
    carrots
¾ cup grated carrot
⅓ cup golden raisins, coarsely chopped
1 teaspoon grated orange peel
1 teaspoon vanilla
2 cups all-purpose flour
¾ cup sugar
1 teaspoon baking soda
1 teaspoon ground cinnamon
¼ cup orange juice
¼ cup toasted pecans, chopped

Preheat oven to 350°F. Grease 13×9-inch baking pan; set aside. Combine milk and butter in large bowl. Add cereal; stand 5 minutes. Add eggs; whisk until blended. Add puréed carrots, grated carrot, raisins, orange peel and vanilla. Stir in flour, sugar, baking soda and cinnamon until well blended. Spread in prepared pan.

Bake 25 minutes or until toothpick inserted in center comes out clean. Insert tines of fork into cake at 1-inch intervals. Spoon orange juice over cake. Sprinkle with pecans; press into cake.

Makes 40 servings

HEATH® Bars

2 packages (8 ounces each) HEATH®
    BITS, divided
1 cup (2 sticks) butter, softened
1 cup packed light brown sugar
1 egg yolk
1 teaspoon vanilla extract
2 cups all-purpose flour
½ cup finely chopped pecans

1. Heat oven to 350°F and set aside ¾ cup Heath Bits.

2. Beat butter in large bowl until creamy; add brown sugar, egg yolk and vanilla; beat until blended. Using spoon, mix in flour, remaining Heath Bits and pecans. Press into ungreased 15½×10½-inch jelly-roll pan.

3. Bake 18 to 20 minutes, or until browned. Remove from oven; immediately sprinkle reserved ¾ cup Heath Bits over top. Cool slightly. Cut into bars while warm. Cool completely. *Makes about 4 dozen bars*

Fruit and Nut Bars

- **1 cup unsifted all-purpose flour**
- **1 cup quick oats**
- **⅔ cup brown sugar**
- **2 teaspoons baking soda**
- **½ teaspoon salt**
- **½ teaspoon cinnamon**
- **⅔ cup buttermilk**
- **3 tablespoons vegetable oil**
- **2 egg whites, lightly beaten**
- **1 Washington Golden Delicious apple, cored and chopped**
- **½ cup dried cranberries or raisins, chopped**
- **¼ cup chopped nuts**
- **2 tablespoons flaked coconut (optional)**

1. Heat oven to 375°F. Lightly grease 9-inch square baking pan. In large mixing bowl, combine flour, oats, brown sugar, baking soda, salt and cinnamon; stir to blend.

2. Add buttermilk, oil and egg whites; beat with electric mixer just until mixed. Stir in apple, dried fruit and nuts; spread evenly in pan and top with coconut, if desired. Bake 20 to 25 minutes or until cake tester inserted in center comes out clean. Cool and cut into 10 bars.

Makes 10 bars

Favorite recipe from **Washington Apple Commission**

Chocolate Iced Shortbread

- **1 cup (2 sticks) butter or margarine, softened**
- **½ cup granulated sugar**
- **1 teaspoon vanilla extract**
- **2 cups all-purpose flour**
- **1¾ cups "M&M's"® Semi-Sweet Chocolate Mini Baking Bits, divided**
- **1 cup prepared chocolate frosting**

Preheat oven to 350°F. Lightly grease 13×9×2-inch baking pan. In large bowl cream butter, sugar and vanilla until light and fluffy. Add flour; mix to form stiff dough. Stir in 1 cup "M&M's"® Semi-Sweet Chocolate Mini Baking Bits. Press dough into prepared pan. Bake 18 to 20 minutes or until firm. Cool completely. Spread with chocolate frosting; sprinkle with remaining ¾ cup "M&M's"® Semi-Sweet Chocolate Mini Baking Bits. Cut into bars. Store in tightly covered container.

Makes 32 bars

Helpful Hint

Cookies, brownies and bars make great gifts. Place them in a paper-lined tin or on a decorative plate; cover with plastic wrap and tie with colorful ribbon. For a special touch, include the recipe.

Polish Honey Bars

- ½ **cup sugar, divided**
- 2 **tablespoons boiling water**
- ⅓ **cup honey**
- 2 **tablespoons butter**
- 1 **teaspoon ground allspice**
- ½ **teaspoon ground cinnamon**
- ¼ **teaspoon ground cloves**
- ¼ **teaspoon ground nutmeg**
- 2 **cups all-purpose flour**
- 3 **tablespoons cold water**
- 1 **large egg**
- 1 **teaspoon baking soda**
  Chocolate Filling (recipe follows)
- 1 **cup semisweet chocolate chips, melted**
- 32 **whole toasted almonds**

1. Stir 2 tablespoons sugar and boiling water in saucepan over medium heat until dissolved and slightly brown. Add remaining sugar, honey, butter and spices; bring to a boil over high heat, stirring constantly. Remove from heat. Pour into bowl; cool. Add flour, cold water, egg and baking soda to bowl; blend well. Cover; stand 20 minutes.

2. Preheat oven to 350°F. Grease and flour 15×10-inch jelly-roll pan. Roll dough on lightly floured surface to almost fit size of pan. Press into pan to edges. Bake 10 to 13 minutes or until cookie base spring back when touched. Remove pan to wire rack; cool completely.

3. Run knife around cookie base edge to loosen. Place wire rack top-side down over pan; flip rack and pan together. Base should drop out of pan onto rack. Cut in half to form 2 rectangles.

4. Prepare Chocolate Filling; spread evenly over 1 rectangle. Top with other rectangle, flat-side up. Wrap cookie sandwich in plastic wrap. Place baking sheet on top of cookie sandwich; place heavy cans or weights on baking sheet to press sandwich layers together. Let stand overnight.

5. When cookie is ready to frost, dip wide part of each almond into melted chocolate; place on waxed paper to set. Remove weights and baking sheet from sandwich; unwrap. Spread remaining chocolate over top. Before chocolate sets, score into 32 bars. Place 1 dipped almond on each bar. Stand until set; cut into bars.   *Makes 32 bars*

Chocolate Filling

- ¼ **cup whipping cream**
- ½ **cup semisweet chocolate chips**
- 1 **cup toasted almonds, ground**
- ¾ **cup powdered sugar, divided**
- ½ **teaspoon vanilla**

Heat cream and chocolate chips in saucepan over medium heat until smooth, stirring constantly. Remove from heat; stir in almonds, ½ cup powdered sugar and vanilla. Stir in additional powdered sugar until stiff enough to spread.

Kringle Cookies

1½ **cups chocolate-covered graham cracker crumbs (about 17 crackers)**
3 **tablespoons butter** *or* **margarine, melted**
1 **package (8 ounces) PHILADELPHIA® Cream Cheese, softened**
½ **cup crunchy peanut butter**
1 **cup powdered sugar**
2 **squares BAKER'S® Semi-Sweet Chocolate**
1 **teaspoon butter** *or* **margarine**

MIX crumbs and melted butter. Press onto bottom of 9-inch square baking pan. Bake at 350°F for 20 minutes. Cool.

BEAT cream cheese, peanut butter and sugar with electric mixer on medium speed until well blended. Spread over crust.

MICROWAVE chocolate with 1 teaspoon butter on HIGH 1 to 2 minutes or until chocolate begins to melt, stirring halfway though heating time. Stir until chocolate is completely melted. Drizzle over cream cheese mixture.

REFRIGERATE 6 hours or overnight. Cut into squares. Store in airtight container in refrigerator.

Makes 18 servings

Lemon-Cranberry Bars

½ **cup frozen lemonade concentrate, thawed**
½ **cup spoonable sugar substitute**
¼ **cup margarine**
1 **egg**
1½ **cups all-purpose flour**
2 **teaspoons grated lemon peel**
½ **teaspoon baking soda**
½ **teaspoon salt**
½ **cup dried cranberries**

1. Preheat oven to 375°F. Lightly coat 8-inch square baking pan with nonstick cooking spray; set aside.

2. Combine lemonade concentrate, sugar substitute, margarine and egg in medium bowl; mix well. Add flour, lemon peel, baking soda and salt; stir well. Stir in cranberries; spoon into prepared pan.

3. Bake 20 minutes or until light brown. Cool completely in pan on wire rack. Cut into 16 squares.

Makes 16 bars

Chocolate Coconut Bars

COOKIE BASE
- ⅔ **cup sugar**
- ½ **Butter Flavor* CRISCO® Stick or ½ cup Butter Flavor CRISCO® all-vegetable shortening plus additional for greasing**
- ¼ **cup cocoa**
- 1 **egg**
- 1 **tablespoon water**
- 1¼ **cups all-purpose flour**
- ¼ **teaspoon salt**

FILLING
- 1 **can (14 ounces) sweetened condensed milk (not evaporated milk)**
- 3 **tablespoons all-purpose flour**
- 1 **teaspoon pure vanilla extract**
- ¾ **cup semi-sweet chocolate chips**
- ⅔ **cup chopped walnuts**
- ½ **cup flake coconut**

*Butter Flavor Crisco is artificially flavored.

1. Heat oven to 350°F. Grease 13×9×2-inch pan with shortening. Place cooling rack on countertop.

2. For cookie base, combine sugar, shortening, cocoa, egg and water in large bowl. Beat at medium speed of electric mixer until well blended.

3. Combine 1¼ cups flour and salt. Add gradually to creamed mixture at low speed. Beat just until blended. Press into bottom of lightly greased pan.

4. Bake at 350°F for 10 minutes. *Do not overbake.*

5. For filling, combine condensed milk, 3 tablespoons flour and vanilla. Stir with spoon until well blended. Stir in chocolate chips, nuts and coconut. Spoon over baked cookie base. Spread carefully to cover.

6. Return to oven. Bake 20 minutes. *Do not overbake.* Remove pan to cooling rack. Cut into bars about 1½×1½ inches.

Makes about 4 dozen bars

Helpful Hint

Rich, buttery bar cookies freeze extremely well. Freeze baked and cooled bar cookies in airtight containers or freezer bags for up to six months. Thaw bar cookies unwrapped at room temperature.

Frosted Peanut Butter Squares

COOKIE BASE

- ½ cup creamy peanut butter
- ⅓ Butter Flavor* CRISCO® Stick or ⅓ cup Butter Flavor CRISCO® all-vegetable shortening plus additional for greasing
- 1½ cups firmly packed light brown sugar
- 2 eggs
- 1½ cups all-purpose flour
- 1½ teaspoons baking powder
- ½ teaspoon salt
- ¼ cup milk
- 1 teaspoon pure vanilla extract

FROSTING

- ⅔ cup creamy peanut butter
- ¼ Butter Flavor CRISCO® Stick or ¼ cup Butter Flavor CRISCO® all-vegetable shortening
- 4 cups confectioners' sugar
- ½ cup milk

DRIZZLE

- ½ cup semi-sweet chocolate chips
- ½ Butter Flavor CRISCO® Stick or ½ teaspoon Butter Flavor CRISCO® all-vegetable shortening

Butter Flavor Crisco is artificially flavored.

1. Heat oven to 350°F. Grease 15×10×1-inch pan with shortening. Place rack on countertop.

2. For cookie base, mix ½ cup peanut butter and ⅓ cup shortening in bowl. Beat until blended. Add brown sugar. Beat until well blended. Beat in eggs. Combine flour, baking powder and salt. Combine ¼ cup milk and vanilla. Add flour mixture and milk mixture alternately to creamed mixture. Beat until well blended. Spread in pan.

3. Bake at 350°F for 18 to 20 minutes or until toothpick inserted in center comes out clean. *Do not overbake.* Remove pan to cooling rack; cool.

4. For frosting, combine ⅔ cup peanut butter and ¼ cup shortening in large bowl. Beat until blended. Add confectioners' sugar and ½ cup milk alternately. Mix until blended. Beat until fluffy. Spread on cooled cookie base.

5. For drizzle, melt chocolate chips and ½ teaspoon shortening.** Drizzle over frosting. Cut into squares. Chill 15 to 20 minutes or until chocolate is set. *Makes 3 dozen squares*

**For melting or drizzling, choose one of these methods. Start with chips and Butter Flavor* Crisco® all-vegetable shortening, then: Place in small microwave-safe measuring cup. Microwave at 50% (MEDIUM). Stir after 1 minute. Repeat until smooth. Drizzle from spoon. OR Place in heavy resealable plastic sandwich bag. Seal. Microwave at 50% (MEDIUM). Check every minute until melted. Knead bag until smooth. Cut tiny tip off corner of bag. Squeeze out to drizzle.

Cranberry Cheese Bars

2 cups all-purpose flour
1½ cups quick-cooking or old-fashioned oats, uncooked
¾ cup plus 1 tablespoon firmly packed light brown sugar, divided
1 cup (2 sticks) butter or margarine, softened
1¾ cups "M&M's"® Chocolate Mini Baking Bits, divided
1 8-ounce package cream cheese
1 14-ounce can sweetened condensed milk
¼ cup lemon juice
1 teaspoon vanilla extract
2 tablespoons cornstarch
1 16-ounce can whole berry cranberry sauce

Preheat oven to 350°F. Lightly grease 13×9×2-inch baking pan; set aside. In large bowl combine flour, oats, ¾ cup sugar and butter; mix until crumbly. Reserve 1½ cups crumb mixture for topping. Stir ½ cup "M&M's"® Chocolate Mini Baking Bits into remaining crumb mixture; press into prepared pan. Bake 15 minutes. Cool completely. In large bowl beat cream cheese until light and fluffy; gradually mix in condensed milk, lemon juice and vanilla until smooth. Pour evenly over crust. In small bowl combine remaining 1 tablespoon sugar, cornstarch and cranberry sauce. Spoon over cream cheese

mixture. Stir remaining 1¼ cups "M&M's"® Chocolate Mini Baking Bits into reserved crumb mixture. Sprinkle over cranberry mixture. Bake 40 minutes. Cool at room temperature; refrigerate before cutting. Store in refrigerator in tightly covered container.   *Makes 32 bars*

Almond Toffee Triangles

Bar Cookie Crust (page 44)
⅓ cup KARO® Light or Dark Corn Syrup
⅓ cup packed brown sugar
3 tablespoons margarine or butter
¼ cup heavy or whipping cream
1½ cups sliced almonds
1 teaspoon vanilla

1. Preheat oven to 350°F. Prepare Bar Cookie Crust.

2. Meanwhile, in medium saucepan combine corn syrup, brown sugar, margarine and cream. Bring to boil over medium heat; remove from heat. Stir in almonds and vanilla. Pour over hot crust; spread evenly.

3. Bake 12 minutes or until set and golden. Cool completely on wire rack. Cut into 2-inch squares; cut diagonally in half for triangles.
Makes about 48 triangles

Holiday Brownies

Minted Chocolate Chip Brownies

- ¾ **cup granulated sugar**
- ½ **cup butter**
- 2 **tablespoons water**
- 1 **cup semisweet chocolate chips or mini semisweet chocolate chips**
- 1½ **teaspoons vanilla**
- 2 **eggs**
- 1¼ **cups all-purpose flour**
- ½ **teaspoon baking soda**
- ½ **teaspoon salt**
- 1 **cup mint chocolate chips**
  Powdered sugar for garnish

Preheat oven to 350°F. Grease 9-inch square baking pan. Combine sugar, butter and water in medium microwavable bowl. Microwave at HIGH 2½ to 3 minutes or until butter is melted. Stir in semisweet chips; stir gently until chips are melted and mixture is well blended. Stir in vanilla; let stand 5 minutes to cool.

Beat eggs into chocolate mixture, one at a time. Combine flour, baking soda and salt in small bowl; add to chocolate mixture. Stir in mint chocolate chips. Spread in prepared pan.

Bake about 25 minutes for fudgy brownies or 30 minutes for cakelike brownies.

Remove pan to wire rack; cool completely. Cut into 2¼-inch squares. Sprinkle with powdered sugar, if desired. *Makes about 16 brownies*

Fabulous Blonde Brownies

- 1¾ **cups all-purpose flour**
- 1 **teaspoon baking powder**
- ¼ **teaspoon salt**
- 1 **cup (6 ounces) white chocolate chips**
- 1 **cup (4 ounces) blanched whole almonds, coarsely chopped**
- 1 **cup English toffee bits**
- ⅔ **cup butter, softened**
- 1½ **cups packed light brown sugar**
- 2 **eggs**
- 2 **teaspoons vanilla**

Preheat oven to 350°F. Grease 13×9-inch baking pan. Combine flour, baking powder and salt in small bowl; mix well. Combine white chocolate, almonds and toffee in medium bowl; mix well.

Beat butter and brown sugar in large bowl until light and fluffy. Beat in eggs and vanilla. Add flour mixture; beat until well blended. Stir in ¾ cup white chocolate mixture. Spread evenly in prepared pan.

Bake 20 minutes. Immediately after removing brownies from oven, sprinkle remaining white chocolate mixture over brownies. Press lightly. Bake 15 to 20 minutes or until toothpick inserted into center comes out clean. Cool brownies completely in pan on wire rack. Cut into 2×1½-inch bars.

Makes 3 dozen brownies

Cappuccino Brownies

- 1 **tablespoon TASTER'S CHOICE® Maragor Bold® freeze dried coffee**
- 2 **teaspoons boiling water**
- 1 **cup (6-ounce package) NESTLÉ® TOLL HOUSE® Semi-Sweet Chocolate Morsels**
- ½ **cup sugar**
- ¼ **cup butter, softened**
- 2 **eggs**
- ¼ **teaspoon cinnamon**
- ½ **cup all-purpose flour**

Preheat oven to 350°F. In cup, combine Taster's Choice® Maragor Bold® freeze dried coffee and water; set aside. Melt over hot (not boiling) water, Nestlé® Toll House® Semi-Sweet Chocolate Morsels; stir until smooth. Set aside. In large bowl, combine sugar and butter; beat until creamy. Add eggs, coffee and cinnamon; beat well. Stir in melted morsels and flour. Spread into foil-lined 8-inch square baking pan. Bake at 350°F for 25 to 30 minutes. Cool completely on wire rack. Cut into 2-inch squares.

Makes about 16 brownies

Almond Brownies

- ½ **cup (1 stick) butter**
- 2 **squares (1 ounce each) unsweetened baking chocolate**
- 2 **large eggs**
- 1 **cup firmly packed light brown sugar**
- ¼ **teaspoon almond extract**
- ½ **cup all-purpose flour**
- 1½ **cups "M&M's"® Chocolate Mini Baking Bits, divided**
- ½ **cup slivered almonds, toasted and divided**
- **Chocolate Glaze (recipe follows)**

Preheat oven to 350°F. Grease and flour 8×8×2-inch baking pan; set aside. In small saucepan melt butter and chocolate over low heat; stir to blend. Remove from heat; let cool. In medium bowl beat eggs and brown sugar until well blended; stir in chocolate mixture and almond extract. Add flour. Stir in 1 cup "M&M's"® Chocolate Mini Baking Bits and ¼ cup almonds. Spread batter evenly in prepared pan. Bake 25 to 28 minutes or until firm in center. Cool completely on wire rack. Prepare Chocolate Glaze. Spread over brownies; decorate with remaining ½ cup "M&M's"® Chocolate Mini Baking Bits and remaining ¼ cup almonds. Cut into bars. Store in tightly covered container.

Makes 16 brownies

Chocolate Glaze: In saucepan over low heat bring 4 teaspoons water and 1 tablespoon butter to a boil. Stir in 4 teaspoons unsweetened cocoa powder. Gradually stir in ½ cup powdered sugar until smooth. Remove from heat and stir in ¼ teaspoon vanilla extract. Let glaze cool slightly.

Frosted Maraschino Brownies

- 24 **red maraschino cherries, drained**
- 1 **(23.6-ounce) package brownie mix, plus ingredients to prepare mix**
- 2 **cups powdered sugar**
- ½ **cup plus 1 tablespoon butter, softened**
- 3 **tablespoons milk**
- 2 **tablespoons instant vanilla pudding mix**
- 1 **ounce sweet baking chocolate**

Preheat oven to temperature directed on brownie mix. Pat cherries dry with paper towel; set aside. Prepare and bake brownies according to package directions for 13×9-inch pan; cool. Beat sugar, ½ cup butter, milk and pudding mix until smooth. Cover; chill until slightly thickened. Spread over brownie in pan. Place cherries on frosting. In saucepan over low heat melt chocolate and remaining 1 tablespoon butter; stir. Cool slightly. Drizzle chocolate mixture over cherries; let set.

Makes 24 brownies

Favorite recipe from **Cherry Marketing Institute**

Fancy Walnut Brownies

BROWNIES
 1 package DUNCAN HINES® Chocolate
  Lovers Walnut Brownie Mix
 1 egg
 ⅓ cup water
 ⅓ cup vegetable oil

GLAZE
 4½ cups confectioners' sugar
 ½ cup milk or water
 24 walnut halves, for garnish

CHOCOLATE DRIZZLE
 ⅓ cup semi-sweet chocolate chips
 1 tablespoon vegetable shortening

1. Preheat oven to 350°F. Place 24 (2-inch) foil cupcake liners on baking sheets.

2. **For brownies,** combine brownie mix, egg, water and oil in large bowl. Stir with spoon until well blended, about 50 strokes. Stir in contents of walnut packet from Mix. Fill foil liners with 2 generous tablespoons batter. Bake at 350°F for 20 to 25 minutes or until set. Cool completely. Remove liners. Turn brownies upside down on cooling rack.

3. **For glaze,** combine confectioners' sugar and milk in medium bowl. Blend until smooth. Spoon glaze over first brownie to completely cover. Top immediately with walnut half. Repeat with remaining brownies. Allow glaze to set.

4. **For chocolate drizzle,** place chocolate chips and shortening in resealable plastic bag; seal. Place bag in bowl of hot water for several minutes. Dry with paper towel. Knead until blended and chocolate is smooth. Snip pinpoint hole in corner of bag. Drizzle chocolate over brownies. Store in single layer in airtight containers. *Makes 24 brownies*

Helpful Hint
Before glazing and drizzling cookies or brownies, place waxed paper under the wire rack to catch the excess and make cleanup easier.

Ornament Brownies

  1 tablespoon freeze dried coffee
  1 tablespoon boiling water
  ¾ cup all-purpose flour
  ¾ teaspoon ground cinnamon
  ½ teaspoon baking powder
  ¼ teaspoon salt
  ½ cup sugar
  ¼ cup butter, softened
  2 large eggs
  **6 squares (1 ounce each) semisweet
      chocolate, melted**
    Prepared vanilla frosting or icing
    Assorted food colors
    **Small candy canes, assorted candies and
      sprinkles for decoration**

1. Preheat oven to 350°F. Grease 8-inch square baking pan; set aside. Dissolve coffee in boiling water in small cup; set aside. Combine flour, cinnamon, baking powder and salt in bowl.

2. Beat sugar and butter in large bowl until light and fluffy. Beat in eggs, 1 at a time, scraping down side of bowl after each addition. Beat in coffee mixture and chocolate until blended. Add flour mixture. Beat until blended, scraping down side of bowl once. Spread batter in prepared pan.

3. Bake 30 to 35 minutes or until center is set. Remove to wire rack; cool completely. Cut into holiday shapes using 2-inch cookie cutters.

4. Tint frosting with food colors to desired color. Spread over each brownie shape. Break off top of small candy cane to create loop. Insert in top of brownie. Decorate with assorted candies and sprinkles as desired. *Makes about 8 brownies*

Derby Brownies

  **1 package DUNCAN HINES® Walnut
      Brownie Mix**
  **½ cup (1 stick) butter or margarine,
      softened**
  **1 pound confectioners' sugar (about 3½ to
      4 cups)**
  2 tablespoons bourbon or milk
  **1 container DUNCAN HINES® Dark
      Chocolate Frosting**

Preheat oven to 350°F. Grease bottom only of 13×9-inch pan.

Prepare brownie mix as directed on package for cake-like brownies. Pour into prepared pan. Bake 24 to 27 minutes or until set. Cool completely in pan. Beat butter until smooth in large mixing bowl; stir in sugar and bourbon. Beat until smooth and of spreading consistency. Spread over brownies; chill. Top with frosting. Chill 2 to 4 hours. Cut into bars and serve at room temperature. *Makes 24 brownies*

Bittersweet Pecan Brownies with Caramel Sauce

BROWNIE
- ¾ **cup all-purpose flour**
- ¼ **teaspoon baking soda**
- 4 **squares (1 ounce each) bittersweet or unsweetened chocolate, coarsely chopped**
- ½ **cup (1 stick) plus 2 tablespoons I CAN'T BELIEVE IT'S NOT BUTTER!® Spread**
- ¾ **cup sugar**
- 2 **eggs**
- ½ **cup chopped pecans**

CARAMEL SAUCE
- ¾ **cup firmly packed light brown sugar**
- 6 **tablespoons I CAN'T BELIEVE IT'S NOT BUTTER!® Spread**
- ⅓ **cup whipping or heavy cream**
- ½ **teaspoon apple cider vinegar or fresh lemon juice**

For brownie, preheat oven to 325°F. Line 8-inch square baking pan with aluminum foil, then grease and flour foil; set aside. In small bowl, combine flour and baking soda; set aside.

In medium microwave-safe bowl, microwave chocolate and I Can't Believe It's Not Butter! Spread at HIGH (Full Power) 1 minute or until chocolate is melted; stir until smooth. With wooden spoon, beat in sugar, then eggs. Beat in flour mixture. Evenly spread into prepared pan; sprinkle with pecans.

Bake 31 minutes or until toothpick inserted in center comes out clean. On wire rack, cool completely. To remove brownies, lift edges of foil. Cut brownies into 4 squares, then cut each square into 2 triangles.

For caramel sauce, in medium saucepan, bring brown sugar, I Can't Believe It's Not Butter! Spread and cream just to a boil over high heat, stirring frequently. Cook 3 minutes. Stir in vinegar. To serve, pour caramel sauce around brownie and top, if desired, with vanilla or caramel ice cream. *Makes 8 servings*

Helpful Hint

Store chocolate in a cool, dry place. If chocolate gets too warm, the cocoa butter rises to the surface and causes a grayish white appearance, which is called a bloom. The bloom will not affect the chocolate's taste or baking quality.

Cream Cheese Swirled Brownies

FILLING

- ⅓ **Butter Flavor* CRISCO® Stick or ⅓ cup Butter Flavor CRISCO® all-vegetable shortening plus additional for greasing**
- 1 **package (8 ounces) cream cheese, softened**
- 1 **teaspoon pure vanilla extract**
- ½ **cup sugar**
- 2 **eggs**
- 3 **tablespoons all-purpose flour**

BROWNIE

- ⅔ **Butter Flavor CRISCO® Stick or ⅔ cup Butter Flavor CRISCO® all-vegetable shortening**
- 4 **squares unsweetened baking chocolate**
- 2 **cups sugar**
- 4 **eggs**
- 1 **teaspoon pure vanilla extract**
- 1¼ **cups all-purpose flour**
- 1 **teaspoon baking powder**
- 1 **teaspoon salt**

*Butter Flavor Crisco is artificially flavored.

1. Heat oven to 350°F. Grease 13×9×2-inch pan with shortening. Place cooling rack on countertop.

2. For filling, combine ⅓ cup shortening, cream cheese and vanilla in small bowl. Beat at medium speed of electric mixer until well blended. Beat in ½ cup sugar. Add 2 eggs, 1 at a time; beat well after each addition. Beat in 3 tablespoons flour.

3. For brownie, melt ⅔ cup shortening and chocolate in large saucepan on low heat. Remove from heat. Stir 2 cups sugar into melted chocolate mixture with spoon. Stir 1 egg at a time quickly into hot mixture. Stir in vanilla.

4. Combine 1¼ cups flour, baking powder and salt. Stir gradually into chocolate mixture.

5. Spread half the chocolate mixture in greased baking pan. Drop cheese mixture over chocolate layer. Spread gently to cover. Drop remaining chocolate mixture over cream cheese layer. Spread gently to cover. Swirl 2 mixtures together using tip of knife.**

6. Bake at 350°F for 35 minutes. *Do not overbake.* Remove pan to cooling rack and cool. Cut into squares about 2×2 inches.

Makes about 2 dozen squares

**A nice swirl design depends on how much you pull knife through batter. Do not overdo.

Oatmeal Brownies

- ⅔ cup granulated sugar
- ⅓ cup water
- 3 tablespoons CRISCO® Oil*
- ½ teaspoon vanilla
- 2 egg whites, lightly beaten
- ½ cup all-purpose flour
- ⅓ cup quick oats (not instant or old fashioned)
- ¼ cup unsweetened cocoa powder
- ¾ teaspoon baking powder
- ⅛ teaspoon salt
- 1 teaspoon confectioners' sugar

Use your favorite Crisco Oil product.

1. Heat oven to 350°F. Oil 8-inch square pan lightly. Place cooling rack on countertop.

2. Combine granulated sugar, water, oil and vanilla in medium bowl. Stir well. Add egg whites. Stir well.

3. Combine flour, oats, cocoa, baking powder and salt. Add to sugar mixture, stirring well. Pour into prepared pan.

4. Bake at 350°F for 23 minutes or until toothpick inserted in center comes out clean. *Do not overbake.* Cool. Sprinkle with confectioners' sugar. Cut into bars.

Makes about 12 brownies

Rocky Road Brownies

- 1 cup HERSHEY'S Semi-Sweet Chocolate Chips
- 1¼ cups miniature marshmallows
- 1 cup chopped nuts
- ½ cup (1 stick) butter or margarine
- 1 cup sugar
- 1 teaspoon vanilla extract
- 2 eggs
- ½ cup all-purpose flour
- ⅓ cup HERSHEY'S Cocoa
- ½ teaspoon baking powder
- ½ teaspoon salt

1. Heat oven to 350°F. Grease 9-inch square baking pan.

2. Stir together chocolate chips, marshmallows and nuts; set aside. Place butter in large microwave safe bowl. Microwave at HIGH (100% power) 1 to 1½ minutes or until melted. Add sugar, vanilla and eggs, beating with spoon until well blended. Add flour, cocoa, baking powder and salt; blend well. Spread batter in prepared pan.

3. Bake 22 minutes. Sprinkle chocolate chip mixture over top. Continue baking 5 minutes or until marshmallows have softened and puffed slightly. Cool completely. With wet knife, cut into squares.

Makes about 20 brownies

Acknowledgments

The publisher would like to thank the companies and organizations listed below for the use of their recipes and photographs in this publication.

Almond Board of California

Bestfoods

Cherry Marketing Institute

DAVIS® Baking Powder

Duncan Hines® and Moist Deluxe® are registered trademarks of Aurora Foods Inc.

Hershey Foods Corporation

Kraft Foods Holdings

Lipton®

©Mars, Inc. 2001

Nestlé USA, Inc.

The Procter & Gamble Company

Sokol and Company

Washington Apple Commission

Index

METRIC CONVERSION CHART

VOLUME MEASUREMENTS (dry)

1/8 teaspoon = 0.5 mL
1/4 teaspoon = 1 mL
1/2 teaspoon = 2 mL
3/4 teaspoon = 4 mL
1 teaspoon = 5 mL
1 tablespoon = 15 mL
2 tablespoons = 30 mL
1/4 cup = 60 mL
1/3 cup = 75 mL
1/2 cup = 125 mL
2/3 cup = 150 mL
3/4 cup = 175 mL
1 cup = 250 mL
2 cups = 1 pint = 500 mL
3 cups = 750 mL
4 cups = 1 quart = 1 L

VOLUME MEASUREMENTS (fluid)

1 fluid ounce (2 tablespoons) = 30 mL
4 fluid ounces (1/2 cup) = 125 mL
8 fluid ounces (1 cup) = 250 mL
12 fluid ounces (1 1/2 cups) = 375 mL
16 fluid ounces (2 cups) = 500 mL

WEIGHTS (mass)

1/2 ounce = 15 g
1 ounce = 30 g
3 ounces = 90 g
4 ounces = 120 g
8 ounces = 225 g
10 ounces = 285 g
12 ounces = 360 g
16 ounces = 1 pound = 450 g

DIMENSIONS

1/16 inch = 2 mm
1/8 inch = 3 mm
1/4 inch = 6 mm
1/2 inch = 1.5 cm
3/4 inch = 2 cm
1 inch = 2.5 cm

OVEN TEMPERATURES

250°F = 120°C
275°F = 140°C
300°F = 150°C
325°F = 160°C
350°F = 180°C
375°F = 190°C
400°F = 200°C
425°F = 220°C
450°F = 230°C

BAKING PAN SIZES

Utensil	Size in Inches/Quarts	Metric Volume	Size in Centimeters
Baking or Cake Pan (square or rectangular)	8×8×2	2 L	20×20×5
	9×9×2	2.5 L	23×23×5
	12×8×2	3 L	30×20×5
	13×9×2	3.5 L	33×23×5
Loaf Pan	8×4×3	1.5 L	20×10×7
	9×5×3	2 L	23×13×7
Round Layer Cake Pan	8×1½	1.2 L	20×4
	9×1½	1.5 L	23×4
Pie Plate	8×1¼	750 mL	20×3
	9×1¼	1 L	23×3
Baking Dish or Casserole	1 quart	1 L	—
	1½ quart	1.5 L	—
	2 quart	2 L	—